Miranda Cosgrove

Katie Franks

PowerKiDS press.

New York

Published in 2009 by The Rosen Publishing Group, Inc.
29 East 21st Street, New York, NY 10010

First Edition

Editor: Nicole Pristash
Book Design: Kate Laczynski
Photo Researcher: Jessica Gerweck

Photo Credits: Cover © Jon Kopaloff/Getty Images, Inc.; pp. 4, 7, 8, 11 © Getty Images, Inc.; pp. 12, 15, 16 © Associated Press; p. 19 © Mike Guastella/Getty Images, Inc.; p. 20 © Chad Buchanan/Getty Images, Inc.

Library of Congress Cataloging-in-Publication Data

Franks, Katie.
  Miranda Cosgrove / Katie Franks.
      p. cm. — (Kid stars!)
  Includes index.
  ISBN 978-1-4042-4466-5 (library binding) ISBN 978-1-4042-4531-0 (pbk)
  ISBN 978-1-4042-4549-5 (6-pack)
  1. Cosgrove, Miranda, 1993– —Juvenile literature. 2. Actors—United States—Biography—Juvenile literature. I. Title.
  PN2287.C634F73 2009
  792.02'8092—dc22
  [B]
                                    2007051793

Manufactured in the United States of America

Contents

Many people who have worked with Miranda say she is not only very talented, but also very grown up for such a young star.

Meet Miranda Cosgrove

Miranda Cosgrove is a talented star in the making. She first became famous by playing the character Summer Hathaway, in the hit movie *School of Rock*. You may have seen her play Drake Bell's sister on the Nickelodeon show *Drake & Josh*, too. Miranda's biggest job yet, however, is starring in her very own show, *iCarly*.

Miranda has been working nearly all her life. Her smart and funny characters have quickly made her a favorite actress among young girls. Let's take a look at the work she has done and what makes her such a great star!

Miranda's Early Years

Miranda Taylor Cosgrove was born on May 14, 1993. She grew up in Los Angeles, California, where Hollywood and many acting jobs are. Growing up in such a great place for actors helped Miranda break into the business.

When Miranda was three years old, a talent **agent** saw her singing and dancing in a Los Angeles **restaurant**. The agent asked Miranda's mother if she thought her daughter would like to act. After thinking about it, Miranda's mother decided to let Miranda try out for **commercials**. Some of Miranda's early commercials were for the restaurant McDonald's and for Mello Yello soda.

Miranda did not plan on becoming an actress. If her agent did not see her singing when she was a child, she might not be the star she is today.

Miranda (front) said that even though she and the other stars of *School of Rock* had to shoot scenes over and over again, Jack Black (back) kept them going.

Looking for a Break

Miranda had fun acting in commercials, but as she got a little older, she wanted to get bigger roles, or parts. To do so, Miranda started trying out for roles in TV shows and movies. In 2001, when she was eight, she got her biggest part yet on the very first **episode** of the TV show *Smallville*.

The next year, Miranda beat out thousands of other kids for the role that would be her big movie break. Her acting and musical talent won her a part in the movie *School of Rock*, with actor Jack Black.

School of Rock

In 2002, Miranda went to New York City to make *School of Rock*. She played Summer Hathaway, the manager of her fourth-grade class band. The band entered a battle of the bands **competition**. As the manager, Summer looked after the band and made sure things got done.

Summer Hathaway was one of the standout characters, and the movie was a big hit. Just as *School of Rock* was playing in **theaters**, Miranda got more good news. A TV show she had just made, called *Drake & Josh*, was going to be on TV!

Miranda said making *School of Rock* was very cool.
Here she is seen with her cast mates at the movie's first
showing on September 24, 2003.

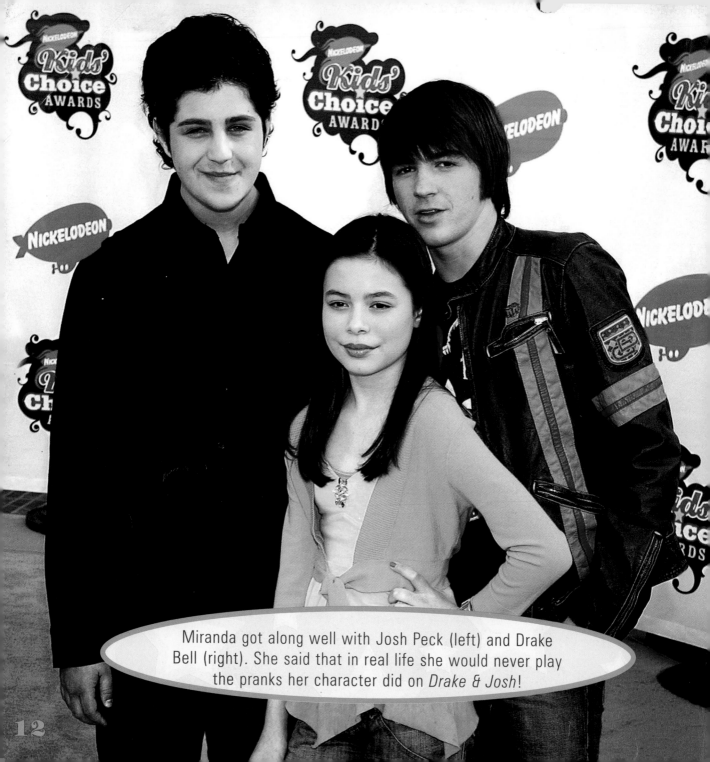

Miranda got along well with Josh Peck (left) and Drake Bell (right). She said that in real life she would never play the pranks her character did on *Drake & Josh*!

When Miranda was 10, *Drake & Josh* began playing on Nickelodeon. Miranda played Drake's younger sister, Megan. Megan liked to play lots of pranks, or jokes, on Drake and Josh. Sometimes, the boys were even a little afraid of Megan and what she might do!

Drake & Josh ran from 2004 until 2007. During this time, Miranda appeared on other **popular** Nickelodeon shows, playing many different characters. Some of those shows were *All That* and *Zoey 101*. Miranda also acted in some movies. She played Joni North, in *Yours, Mine, and Ours*, a movie about a family with 18 children!

Making iCarly

After *Drake & Josh* ended, the show's producers decided to make another show for Nickelodeon and have Miranda star in it. In the new show, called *iCarly*, Miranda plays 13-year-old Carly Shay. She lives in Seattle, Washington, with her older brother Spencer, who is an artist.

In the show, Carly puts a **webcast** on the **Internet** with her best friend, Sam. The webcast includes videos sent in by young people, in which they sing, dance, or do whatever they want to do. Carly starts the webcast so that kids can have a place to show off their talents.

Miranda's character on *iCarly* does a lot of silly things. Here Miranda is seen playing with paint and making a mess on the set of the show.

Miranda has to memorize, or remember, many lines for each episode of *iCarly*. Here she is getting help practicing her lines with her cast mates.

A Hit Show

iCarly was a hit from its very first episode. About three and a half **million** people tune in every week! The cool thing about this show is that it sometimes uses videos sent in by *iCarly*'s own viewers! *iCarly* is the first **scripted** show to use videos sent in by kids.

iCarly fans can go to the show's web site and send in videos of themselves. In the first few months after the show started, viewers sent in more than 10,000 videos! Miranda says that for her, the coolest part of doing the show is watching all of them.

A Rising Star

Miranda has had a lot of success very early in life. Along with two hit TV shows and a hit movie, she has also been **nominated** for many **awards**. Miranda was nominated along with her cast mates for an MTV Movie Award for *School of Rock*. For *Yours, Mine, and Ours*, Miranda was nominated for a Young Artist Award. She was also nominated for a Young Artist Award for *Drake & Josh*!

Miranda keeps a cool head about fame, though. She says that Drake and Josh have told her to be herself and enjoy her success.

In this photo, Miranda is signing a book for one of her fans. Miranda said that the weirdest thing a fan has asked her to sign is a sock!

Miranda loves acting and wants to keep doing it. However, she wants to finish school, too.

What's Next?

Drake & Josh and *iCarly* have made Miranda Cosgrove a popular star. Kids everywhere are starting to know who she is. Her fans cannot wait to see what else she will do. What is next for this bright, young talent?

Besides *iCarly*, Miranda is also working on her studies. Like many kid stars, Miranda had her own teacher to help her with her schooling. Now, she does her schoolwork on the Internet. Miranda hopes to do more movies when she has the time, but for now she is having a great time starring in her own show!

MIRANDA COSGROVE

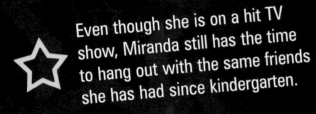

 Even though she is on a hit TV show, Miranda still has the time to hang out with the same friends she has had since kindergarten.

 Miranda enjoys reading.

 She is 5 feet 4 inches (1.63 m) tall.

 Miranda sings the opening song for *iCarly*. Drake Bell sings backup on the song.

Two of Miranda's favorite actresses are Reese Witherspoon and Rachel McAdams.

 She loves to ride horses.

 Miranda writes in her journal every day.

 Miranda is a little bit like Carly. She likes to make videos of herself singing and playing around.

 Along with playing his sister on *Drake & Josh*, Miranda also played Drake Bell's younger sister in the 2005 movie *Yours, Mine, and Ours*.

 Miranda's favorite colors are pink and green.

Glossary

agent (AY-jent) A person who helps an actress with her job.

awards (uh-WORDZ) Special honors given to someone.

commercials (kuh-MER-shulz) TV or radio messages trying to sell something.

competition (kom-pih-TIH-shun) A game.

episode (EH-puh-sohd) One show of a TV show's run.

Internet (IN-ter-net) A network that ties computers around the world together and supplies facts.

million (MIL-yun) A very large number.

nominated (NAH-muh-nayt-ed) To have someone suggest that you be given an award.

popular (PAH-pyuh-lur) Liked by lots of people.

restaurant (RES-tuh-rahnt) A place where food is made and served.

scripted (SKRIPT-ed) Having a written story.

theaters (THEE-uh-turz) Buildings where plays and movies are shown.

webcast (WEB-kast) A short show or movie shown on the Internet.

Index

A
actress(es), 5, 22
agent, 6

C
commercials, 6, 9

D
Drake & Josh, 5, 10,
    13–14, 18, 21–22

E
episode, 9, 17

I
iCarly, 5, 14, 17,
    21–22

M
movie(s), 5, 9–10,
    13, 18, 21–22

S
School of Rock, 5,
    9–10, 18
sister, 5, 13, 22

T
theaters, 10

W
webcast, 14

Web Sites

Due to the changing nature of Internet links, PowerKids Press has developed an online list of Web sites related to the subject of this book. This site is updated regularly. Please use this link to access the list:
www.powerkidslinks.com/kids/mircos/